THE WISDOM OF DESMOND TUTU

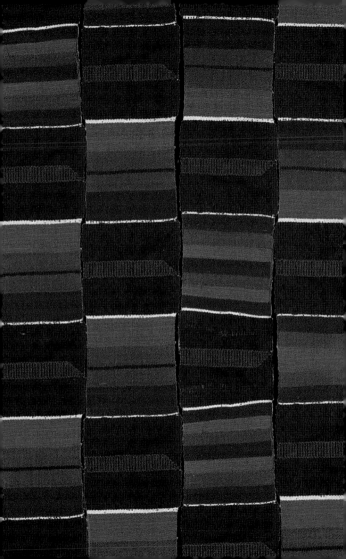

THE
WISDOM
OF
Desmond Tutu

COMPILED BY
MICHAEL BATTLE

Westminster John Knox Press
Louisville, Kentucky

Text © 1998.
Original edition published in English under the title
The Wisdom of Desmond Tutu by Lion Publishing plc, Oxford,
England. Copyright © Lion Publishing plc 1998.

Design by Philippa Jenkins
Cover and first page illustration by David Axtell

Published by Westminster John Knox Press, 2000
Louisville, Kentucky

00 01 02 03 04 05 06 07 08 09 -- 10 9 8 7 6 5 4 3 2 1

A catalog card for this book may be obtained
from the Library of Congress

ISBN 0-664-22210-2

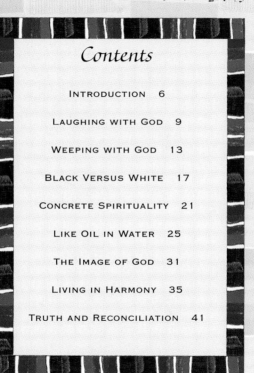

Contents

Archbishop Desmond Tutu is renowned worldwide for his work towards reconciliation and peace in twentieth-century South Africa. In the midst of a world of pain and violence, Tutu's life has been consistently creative and inspirational – from his protests and action against an unjust apartheid government to his role as head of the Truth and Reconciliation Commission which seeks restorative justice in South Africa and the world.

I first met Archbishop Desmond Tutu in 1993, when I arrived for what was to be a two-year stay in South Africa. Being keenly interested in Tutu's theology, I had made it the subject of my PhD. I had been granted access to the Archbishop's unpublished writings and speeches, and was able to help with the work of collecting and referencing some of this material. This has allowed me an invaluable insight into the man and his work.

It is clear that Tutu's theology and spirituality are inseparable from his political life – a response to the powerful Afrikaaner doctrine of apartheid which was enacted in South African law in 1948, but which had been a concrete reality for many decades before that. Tutu's beliefs have consistently been refined by the need to act within this context, and his actions have stemmed directly from his beliefs.

As Africans confront the dilemma of an identity shaped largely by European attitudes and perceptions, Tutu's spirituality displays an alternative reality – one which goes beyond the boundaries of nationalism. For Tutu, I believe, draws upon not only his deep Christian faith and the traditions of the worldwide Anglican church, but also upon the distinct African concept of 'ubuntu', which recognizes the fundamental interdependence of people. And for Tutu, who you are to a large extent determines what you see and how you see it.

Tutu's approach of mediation and acceptance in the face of conflict is combined with a belief in the classical Christian doctrine of the Trinity – a belief that, at the very heart of the universe, there is a relationship of love, equality and interdependence. This belief leaves no place for the supremacy of one race above another – and insists that all peoples belong to a global family.

And so Tutu works towards the transformation of human relationships and political realities, his theology matched by a profound spirituality and practicality, as well as a personal warmth and a wonderful sense of humour. This small volume seeks to provide a glimpse into the wisdom that Desmond Tutu has brought to one of the most complex situations of the modern world. For those who wish to read further, I have included a short booklist overleaf.

MICHAEL BATTLE

FURTHER READING

Michael Battle, *Reconciliation: The Ubuntu Theology of Desmond Tutu*, Pilgrim Press, 1997.

Shirley Du Boulay, *Tutu: Voice of the Voiceless*, London: Hodder and Stoughton, 1988.

Desmond Tutu, *An African Prayer Book*, New York: Doubleday, 1995.

– *Crying in the Wilderness*, Grand Rapids: Eerdmans, 1982.

– *Hope and Suffering*, Grand Rapids: Eerdmans, 1984.

– *The Rainbow People of God: The Making of a Peaceful Revolution*, ed. John Allen, New York: Doubleday, 1994.

Laughing
with God

THE AUDIENCE HAD A
WONDERFUL CAPACITY
TO LAUGH... IT SEEMED
EXTRAORDINARY, THIS
GIFT OF LAUGHTER IN
THE MIDST OF SO MUCH
ANGUISH. PERHAPS, AS
HAS SOMETIMES BEEN
REMARKED, WE LAUGH
ONLY BECAUSE IF WE
DID NOT, WE WOULD
CRY AND CRY.

'FOREWORD', IN *NELSON MANDELA*

The story is told of how a black man took God to task for creating him black. He really was incensed and exclaimed, 'What sort of colour do you think this is – swarthy and totally unattractive? And just look at my hair – what is this crop of crinkly peppercorns?... I don't like what you have done.' When he had finished his tirade a booming voice responded, 'My son, I placed you in my beautiful garden of Eden, Africa. Can you imagine what would have happened to you if you had had flowing locks, how would you have run like a gazelle in my thick African forests? Your hair would have been caught in the tree branches.' The black man said, 'God, please may I say something?' And God said, 'Yes.' The black man said, 'I'm in North Carolina.'

'SCAPE-GOATISM'

Jesus must have a sense of humour. That is a statement which shocks some people, but can you imagine he would have been able to attract young people, as he seemed to have, if he was humourless? Some of the stories he told were meant to point up a ridiculous feature in our conduct intended to make his audience laugh – like the fellow who is determined to remove a speck of dust from his brother's eye when all along he is sporting an almighty beam sticking out of his own.

But I think Jesus had another brand of humour – when he turned upside down our normal standards and showed that the standards of the Kingdom were somewhat different. It was not the pompous and properly religious Pharisee who would be pleasing to God, but the publican who could not so much as lift his eyes to heaven. The prostitute quite unthinkably might precede the religious leaders into heaven…

So here he comes as a King, hailed by the people in procession, come as they hoped to rid them of the Roman yoke of oppression… riding on an ass…

'PASSIONTIDE, PALM SUNDAY'

I really have virtually nothing new to say... I am beginning to feel like that Professor who had one brilliant speech which he delivered every time he was called to speak. He had got quite bored himself, so he told his driver about his predicament – that he was due to deliver his only speech for the umpteenth time and he was sick to death with it. His driver told him that he already knew the speech word for word as he had listened to it so often. So they checked out and found that the driver was word perfect and he had the right gestures and intonation. So they exchanged roles. The speech had to run exactly thirty minutes and no time must be left over for questions for obvious reasons. The driver/speaker delivered his speech and it was a scintillating success but they had somehow miscalculated and there were two minutes left over and someone asked the inevitable question. And the driver without batting an eyelid said, 'Oh that really is too simple a question. Even my driver sitting at the back there can answer it.'

'THE STATE OF THE NATION'

Weeping
with God

GOD, MY FATHER,
I AM FILLED
WITH ANGUISH AND
PUZZLEMENT.
WHY, OH GOD, IS
THERE SO MUCH
SUFFERING, SUCH
NEEDLESS SUFFERING?
EVERYWHERE WE LOOK
THERE IS PAIN
AND SUFFERING.

'LAMENT FROM AFRICA'

Sometimes you look on and you are filled, maybe, with despair and then you remember that Jesus was strung up on a cross on a Good Friday and nothing could have looked more helpless than a Jesus hung from the cross and a deep darkness covering the face of the earth. Then Easter happened and you are able to say, 'Whammo, hey life is stronger than death.' Light is stronger than darkness, love stronger than hatred, goodness stronger than evil, justice stronger than oppression and injustice and we are able to declare that God's intention for his world is that all of this ugliness must be transformed and transfigured, that there will be peace, that there will be joy, that there will be laughter, that there will be fellowship and reconciliation.

BIRMINGHAM CATHEDRAL ADDRESS

True reconciliation does not mean crying, 'Peace, peace' where there is no peace. No, it is to confront people with the demands of the Gospel of Jesus Christ for justice and peace and compassion and caring. It means taking sides on behalf of the weak and the downtrodden – the least of Christ's brethren – to be the voice of the voiceless ones. You can't be neutral in a situation of injustice and oppression and exploitation.

Be careful if you say you want reconciliation and you are a minister of reconciliation; be sure you know what you are about because reconciliation involves suffering and even death. Reconciliation cannot happen apart from the cross. A Christian who does not suffer for Christ's sake and for the Kingdom's sake can't be a Christian. That is not Desmond Tutu speaking. Actually it is what Jesus himself said: 'Unless you take up your cross and follow me you cannot be my disciple.'

'THE CHURCH AND RECONCILIATION IN SOUTH AFRICA'

RELIGION

Someone has said 'Religion is what you do with your solitude'; perhaps we should say 'Religion is what you do with suffering, yours and that of others.'

'GOD WHO IS THERE'

Religion is not necessarily a good thing. It depends; religion can lead to great good, but it can equally lead to unspeakable evil and suffering.

'THE SECULAR STATE AND RELIGIONS'

Black Versus White

OUR SURVIVAL IS
TOGETHER, BLACK AND
WHITE. OUR HUMANITY IS
CAUGHT UP IN THAT OF
ONE ANOTHER, BLACK
AND WHITE TOGETHER.
THE ONLY WAY WE CAN
BE FREE IS TOGETHER,
BLACK AND WHITE.
THE ONLY WAY WE CAN
BE PEOPLE IS TOGETHER,
BLACK AND WHITE.

'POSTSCRIPT: TO BE HUMAN
IS TO BE FREE'

Y ou whites brought us the Bible; now we blacks are taking it seriously. We are involved with God to set us free from all that enslaves us and makes us less than what he intended us to be. I will demonstrate that apartheid, separate development – or whatever it is called – is evil, totally and without remainder, that it is unchristian and unbiblical. If anyone were to show me otherwise, I would burn my Bible and cease to be a Christian.

Sparks

We will not be seduced by concessions, however massive, through being co-opted into a middle class that must serve as a buffer between affluent and privileged whites and a horde of dispossessed and poor blacks – concessions which would enable those lucky blacks to benefit from the core economy and thus be supporters of the status quo whilst the vast majority of their brothers and sisters are consigned to the outer darkness of unviable Bantustans* where there is poverty and starvation, so that they are reservoirs of cheap labour.

ADDRESS TO THE PRETORIA PRESS CLUB

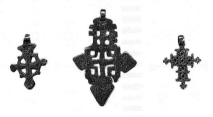

* *reservations*

God was always on the side of the oppressed and exploited, not because they are morally better than their oppressors. No, he is on their side simply and solely because they are oppressed. He wants them to be fully human. And when he liberates the oppressed he also liberates the oppressor, because whites in South Africa will never be truly free until all of us are free.

'GREETINGS FROM BISHOP TUTU
TO THE SOWETO STUDENTS'

Concrete Spirituality

I COULD NOT SURVIVE
AT ALL IF I DID NOT
WORSHIP, IF I DID NOT
MEDITATE, IF I DID NOT
TRY TO HAVE THOSE
MOMENTS OF QUIET TO
BE WITH THE LORD...
I WOULD COLLAPSE...
IT IS THAT BASIC FOR
ME — A VERITABLE
PHYSICAL THING.

'WHERE IS NOW THY GOD?'

FAITH IN ACTION

Those who hope that we will be praying for peace and justice as we assuredly have been and will continue to do are under the false illusion that this means we will be concentrating on otherworldly concerns dealing with purely spiritual and therefore nebulous entities. They have reckoned without the verities of biblical faith... Our faith is embarrassingly concrete, material, real, and incarnational.

SERMON COMMEMORATING A STUDENT UPRISING

Sometimes you may not feel like praying because your prayers are insipid. There is dryness, and God seems miles and miles away. But because you are faithful, you say to God, 'I want to pray, and I will offer you these thirty minutes, God, even if it means fighting these awkward distractions for a few minutes.'

And because you are faithful, someone in South Africa suddenly receives an excess of grace; inexplicably it appears. Perhaps he is in a solitary confinement cell; perhaps he is being tortured. And instead of being hate-filled and embittered, he is able to say, 'You know... when these men are applying their third-degree methods on you, you look on them and say, "These are God's children and they are behaving like animals. They need us to help them recover the humanity they have lost."' How is that possible except that you here have prayed him into the state of grace?

SERMON AT THE WASHINGTON NATIONAL CATHEDRAL

I was blessed in that I had been trained for the priesthood by a religious community, the Community of the Resurrection, who taught us more by example than by precept that the spiritual was absolutely crucial to an authentic Christian existence. I have been brought up on a fare of frequent (often daily) Eucharists, prayer, meditation and Bible study. Our Lord, whom we seek to follow, often spent whole nights in prayer to prepare himself for the arduous work of the Kingdom. There was a clear rhythm to his life, of involvement and withdrawal, of action and retreat... Our action was the direct consequence of our encounter with our Lord and Saviour Jesus Christ, and so we could not understand the familiar dichotomies between the secular and the sacred, the profane and the holy, between religion and politics. It was all a consequence of taking seriously the incarnation, that God had become a real human being of flesh and blood, and everything that affected human life was important to God.

'CHURCH AND PROPHECY IN SOUTH AFRICA TODAY'

Like Oil
in Water

WHY DOES THE CRY 'DON'T MIX RELIGION WITH POLITICS' HAVE SUCH A LONG PEDIGREE?

'THE THEOLOGIAN AND THE GOSPEL OF FREEDOM'

Christianity can never be a personal matter. It has public consequences and we must make public choices. Many people think Christians should be neutral or that the Church must be neutral. But in a situation of injustice and oppression such as we have in South Africa, not to choose to oppose is in fact to have chosen to side with the powerful, with the exploiter, with the oppressor.

'RACISM. WE NEED A PROPHET'

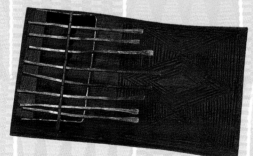

What religious persons bring to bear on any situation are the moral and ethical values enshrined in their faith; and as all human systems are bound to fall short in varying degrees of the absolute standards of the Gospel, so persons of faith will want to support that political system or proposal which, in their view, most approximates those standards on the nature of human community. They will ask how consistent a specific system or plan is with the imperatives of the Gospel of our Lord Jesus Christ; consequently their involvement in socio-political and economic affairs will be dictated by the constraints of the Gospel, and not by political, or other, ideologies.

'THE THEOLOGIAN AND THE GOSPEL OF FREEDOM'

I doubt that there will ever be a genuinely secular society in Africa. For the African the spiritual realm has an abiding reality, and belief in the supernatural – in a God – is something we Africans appear to take in with our mother's milk. Hence communism as dialectical materialism can never satisfy the deep yearnings of the African psyche. An African atheistic materialist is, I am sure, a contradiction in terms. Otherwise there would have been far more Marxist and communist nations in Africa, considering the way previous colonial history favoured the possibility of communist take-overs.

'CALLED TO UNITY AND FELLOWSHIP'

AN ESSENTIAL UNITY

God does not permit me to luxuriate in
narcissistic navel-gazing. For my part, I must
concur with Kenneth Leech in *The Social God* when
he declares that there is an essential unity between
contemplation and action, between prayer and
politics, and between spirituality and justice. It is
a shame that we have to use the conjunction 'and'
when we speak of these things, because for me
they are not separate. Spirituality is justice. My
involvement flows, I hope, from my religion.
That seems to be the case in the Bible. In the life
of Our Lord there was no essential distinction
between the two. Whenever religion rings true,
I find no contradiction.

'WHERE IS NOW THY GOD?'

How do you balance the spiritual and the political aspects of your life?... I do not have a sense of tension between the two. I have come to learn that spirituality is absolutely essential to an authentic Christian life. That is how it was with almost all God's servants. Their encounters with God were not for their own self-aggrandizement but for the sake of others. You meet God as a burning bush in order to be sent to Pharaoh to redeem captives.

'A PRISONER OF HOPE'

The Image of God

... AND SINCE TONIGHT
I AM BEING HONOURED
AS A THEOLOGIAN
I WOULD SAY
APARTHEID MAKES NO
THEOLOGICAL SENSE
EITHER, FOR IT DENIES
THAT HUMAN BEINGS
ARE CREATED IN THE
IMAGE OF GOD.

RESPONSE AT GRADUATION
OF COLUMBIA UNIVERSITY'S
HONORARY DOCTORATE

Apartheid says what makes us valuable in the sight of God is a biological attribute, and by that criterion it talks about something that cannot be universal. If your value depends on something like the colour of your skin, it means that not everybody can have the same value. That is contrary – totally contrary – to the scriptures, which say our value is because we are created in the image of God.

THE RISE OF CHRISTIAN CONSCIENCE

The very hairs of our heads are numbered and we are known by name by this God for whom not even a sparrow can fall to the ground without God noting it. This is tremendous news to those who are downtrodden and oppressed. They discover that they do, indeed, matter enormously to this God. That they have infinite worth in God's sight. For they were created in God's image. This news becomes subversive, explosive, revolutionary material in a situation of injustice and oppression. Why, you tell those who have been marginalized and treated as if they did not count, that they matter, that nothing anybody else does to them can alter the most fundamental fact about them. That God loves them...

'WHERE IS NOW THY GOD?'

PARTNERS WITH GOD

All of us together, black and white, can live in a new society where people count, not because of the colour of their skin or their race but people count because they are created in the image of God, where people can live together as family as God intended and cannot frustrate God's purposes for ever. So God says, 'Will you, and you, and you join me to be my partners to help me to bring about all of this? Will you? Will you be my partner? Will you be my fellow-worker? Will you help me to change the ugliness, the hatred, the anxiety, the fear, the separation, the hunger, the war, the death, the destruction? Will you help me to change it?'

BIRMINGHAM CATHEDRAL ADDRESS

Living in Harmony

... MY EXISTENCE
IS CAUGHT UP AND
INEXTRICABLY BOUND
UP WITH YOURS...
A SOLITARY
HUMAN BEING IS
A CONTRADICTION
IN TERMS.

HANDWRITTEN ADDRESSES AND
SPEECHES, MOREHOUSE MEDICAL
SCHOOL COMMENCEMENT

BEING HUMAN

Let me tell you of something else that belongs to you in your rich African heritage. Back home we speak about something which is very difficult to translate into English. It is called Ubuntu or Botho. It is the essence of being human. It speaks about that which we are aware when you don't have it. You can be wealthy in material goods but you could still be without Ubuntu – for it is a deeply spiritual thing and not dependent on material possessions. It speaks about hospitality, an open and welcoming attitude that is willing to share, to be generous and caring... We say a person is a person through other persons. We don't come fully formed into the world. We learn how to think, how to walk, how to speak, how to behave – indeed how to be human – from other human beings. We need other human beings in order to be human. We are made for togetherness, we are made for family, for fellowship, to exist in a tender network of interdependence.

HANDWRITTEN ADDRESSES AND SPEECHES,
MOREHOUSE MEDICAL SCHOOL COMMENCEMENT

We find that we are placed in a delicate network of vital relationship with the Divine, with my fellow human beings and with the rest of creation...

We are meant then to live as members of one family, the human family, exhibiting a rich diversity of attributes and gifts in our differing cultures as members of different races and coming from different milieus – and precisely because of this diversity, made for interdependence... the peace we want is something positive and dynamic. In the Hebrew it is called shalom, which refers to wholeness, integrity; it means well being, physical and spiritual. It means the abundance of life which Jesus Christ promised he had brought. It has all to do with a harmonious coexistence with one's neighbours in a wholesome environment allowing persons to become more fully human.

'THE QUEST FOR PEACE'

TOTAL BEAUTY

Have you seen a symphony orchestra? They are all dolled up and beautiful with their magnificent instruments, cellos, violins, etc. Sometimes dolled up as the rest, is a chap at the back carrying a triangle. Now and again the conductor will point to him and he will play 'ting'. That might seem so insignificant, but in the conception of the composer something irreplaceable would be lost to the total beauty of the symphony if that 'ting' did not happen.

'WHAT JESUS MEANS TO ME'

God has a dream. God's dream is that his children and the whole of his created order will live in an unbroken harmony. God longs for us all to enjoy shalom, wholeness, prosperity, love and laughter, joy and humanness, compassion and caring, reconciliation, freedom, justice and fellowship. God enlists you and me and all of us to be his fellow workers, agents of transformation, agents for transfiguration, to transform, transfigure all the ugliness of this world, to help God realize his dream so that the kingdoms of this world would become the Kingdom of our God and his Christ and he shall reign for ever and ever. Amen.

'POSTSCRIPT: TO BE HUMAN IS TO BE FREE'

God's purpose is to unite all the separate and divided things and peoples of this world... We are his agents, his instruments; and if we are faithful we will help to bring to pass that great vision of John the Divine – of people from every race, tribe, nation and language united in the praise and worship of Almighty God.

'CALLED TO UNITY AND FELLOWSHIP'

Truth and Reconciliation

JESUS CHRIST
CAME TO EFFECT
RECONCILIATION
BETWEEN US AND GOD
AND BETWEEN US AND
OUR NEIGHBOURS...
RECONCILIATION
IS NEVER CHEAP.
IT COST GOD THE
DEATH OF HIS SON.

ADDRESS, NATIONAL DAY
OF PRAYER

We, the Church of this Jesus Christ, must beware that we don't set up barriers separating and dividing people into those who are inside and those who are outside. We are not God and don't know who is going to heaven and who to hell. Only God knows that... Our business should be to respond to the love of God, to become more and more like God, who lets his sun shine on all and his rain fall for all. We must be Christ-like, compassionate and open, inviting all to come to Christ by the beauty and attractiveness of our lives.

SERMON AT ST AIDAN'S, LANSDOWNE

Until fairly recently, the African Christian has suffered from a form of religious schizophrenia. With part of himself he has been compelled to pay lip service to Christianity as understood, expressed and preached by the white man. But with an ever greater part of himself, a part he has been often ashamed to acknowledge openly and which he has struggled to repress, he has felt that his Africanness was being violated. The white man's largely cerebral religion was hardly touching the depths of his African soul; he was being redeemed from sins he did not believe he had committed; he was being given answers, and often splendid answers, to questions he had not asked.

'WHITHER AFRICAN THEOLOGY?'

These persons tend to have an attenuated doctrine of reconciliation and want to avoid confrontation at all costs – to speak about a neutral God in situations of conflict, of injustice and oppression. They say God does not take sides and so the Church should not take sides, but must be somewhere in the middle. In an attempt to exercise a ministry of reconciliation such people present reconciliation as an easy option for Christians, and they speak about the need to be forgiving, especially to the victims of injustice, without making a call for repentance by the perpetrators of the injustice and for a redress of the unjust system – they will do this to such an extent that profound Christian words such as 'reconciliation' and 'forgiveness' are rejected with contempt by the poor and exploited because they appear to want them to acquiesce in their condition of oppression and exploitation and powerlessness.

HOPE AND SUFFERING

COLD COMFORT

We must be duly mollified and suitably humble and modest in our claims as we look at the track record of the Church and Christianity over the past several centuries of their existence. We should all be appalled, as I am sure we are, as we survey the casualties and shipwrecks that lie strewn all over the landscape. It is true that all the horrendous things that stand as stark monuments to the ghastly things that human beings are capable of in their inhumanity to their fellows are due to the adherents of Christianity falling disgracefully short of the high ideals of their faith. When their practice has been woefully inconsistent with their profession, when what they have been and what they have done, to paraphrase Emerson, have been so loud that you could not hear what they were saying. That, sadly, has been cold comfort. We must start being genuinely penitent; then we might just manage to accomplish something worthwhile as we strive after the high ideals which are at the heart of our faith.

'POSTSCRIPT: TO BE HUMAN IS TO BE FREE'

We should not be surprised that evil can only be maintained by evil. It cannot survive except by propagating more evil. But the point about our faith is that God takes something that was an instrument of evil, of death, of destruction, of shame – the cross – God takes that and transfigures it so that it becomes a source of light.

STATEMENT ON THE DEATH OF
JENNY CURTIS AND HER DAUGHTER

Part 1 quote: Desmond Tutu, 'Foreword', Mary Benson, *Nelson Mandela: The Man and the Movement*, copyright 1994, 1986 Mary Benson, New York: W.W. Norton and Company, Inc. Reprinted by permission.

Extract 1: Desmond Tutu, 'Scape-Goatism', Cape Press Club, 17 March 1987.

Extract 2: Desmond Tutu, Sermon, 'Passiontide, Palm Sunday', undated handwritten text delivered in South Africa in the 1980s.

Extract 3: Desmond Tutu, Address, 'The State of the Nation', Mirge, Cape Town, 1 December 1982.

Part 2 quote: Desmond Tutu, 'Lament from Africa', *Praying for Peace*, compiled by Michael H. Duke, London: Fount Paperbacks, 1991, pp. 63–64.

Extracts 4 and 20: Desmond Tutu, Address, Birmingham Cathedral, pp. 5–6.

Extract 5: Desmond Tutu, Address, 'The Church and Reconciliation in South Africa', P.E. Synod, June 1981.

Extract 6a: Desmond Tutu, Handwritten Address, 'God Who is There', National Christian Youth Convention, Australia, 1987.

Extract 6b: Desmond Tutu, Address on Inter-Faith Relations, 'The Secular State and Religions', Archbishop Stephen Naidoo Memorial Lecture, 8 July 1992.

Part 3 quote and extracts 24 and 29: Desmond Tutu, 'Postscript: To Be Human is to Be Free', *Christianity and Democracy in Global Context*, ed. John Witte, Jr, Boulder: Westview Press, 1993, pp. 313, 320, 311.

Extract 7: Quoted in *The Mind of South Africa*, by Allister Sparks, New York: Ballantine Books, 1990, p. 289. Reprinted by permission of Random House, UK.

Extract 8: Desmond Tutu, Address, The Pretoria Press Club, 4 August 1980.

Extract 9: 'Greetings from Bishop Tutu to the Soweto Students, 16 June 1977', *Pro Veritate*, June 1977, p. 6, quoted in *Church Versus State in South Africa*, p. 213.

Part 4 quote, extracts 16 and 19: Desmond Tutu, Address, 'Where is Now Thy God?', Trinity Institute, New York, 8 January 1989.

Extract 10: Desmond Tutu, handwritten sermon commemorating a student uprising, St George's Cathedral, 16 June 1986.

Extract 11: Desmond Tutu, Sermon at the Washington National Cathedral in Washington D.C., 2 December 1987, *The Rise of Christian Conscience: The Emergence of a Dramatic Renewal Movement in the Church Today*, ed. Jim Wallis, San Francisco: Harper & Row, 1987, p. 60.

Extract 12: Desmond Tutu, 'Church and Prophecy in South Africa Today',

Essex Papers in Theology and Society, Centre for the Study of Theology in the University of Essex, 1991, pp. 16–17.

Part 5 quote and extract 14: Desmond Tutu, 'The Theologian and the Gospel of Freedom', *The Trial of Faith: Theology and the Church Today*, ed. Peter Eaton, West Sussex, England: Churchman Publishing, 1988, pp. 53, 61.

Extract 13: Desmond Tutu in interview with James S. Murray, 'Racism. We need a prophet', *The Australian*, 10 May 1984.

Extracts 15 and 25: Desmond Tutu, 'Called to Unity and Fellowship', The Church and the Alternative Society: Papers and Resolutions of the Eleventh National Conference of the South African Council of Churches, Hammanskraal, 23–27 July 1979, ed. M. Nash, Johannesburg: South African Council of Churches, 1979, pp. 20, 25.

Extract 17: Desmond Tutu, 'A Prisoner of Hope', *Christianity Today*, 5 October 1992, p. 40.

Part 6 quote: Desmond Tutu, Address, 'Response at Graduation of Columbia University's Honorary Doctorate', Presented by Columbia's President at the University of the Witwatersrand, 2 August 1982.

Extract 18: Desmond Tutu in interview with Jim Wallis, *The Rise of Christian Conscience: The Emergence of a Dramatic Renewal Movement in the Church Today*, ed. Jim Wallis, San Francisco: Harper & Row, 1987, p. 58.

Part 7 quote and extract 21: Desmond Tutu, Handwritten Addresses and Speeches, Morehouse Medical School Commencement.

Extract 22: Desmond Tutu, Address, 'The Quest for Peace', Johannesburg, August 1986.

Extract 23: Desmond Tutu, 'What Jesus Means to Me', Durban University, 6–7 August 1981.

Part 8 quote: Desmond Tutu, Address, National Day of Prayer, St George's Cathedral, 5 June 1992.

Extract 26: Desmond Tutu, Handwritten Sermon, St Aidan's, Lansdowne, Sunday, 8 August 1993.

Extract 27: Desmond Tutu, 'Whither African Theology?', *Christianity in Independent Africa*, eds Edward Fasholé, Richard Gray, Adrian Hastings and Godwin Tasie, London: Rex Collings, 1978, p. 366.

Extract 28: Desmond Tutu, *Hope and Suffering*, London: HarperCollins publishers Ltd, p. 38. Reprinted by permission.

Extract 30: Desmond Tutu, Statement, South African Council of Churches General Conference, on the death of Jenny Curtis and her daughter, 29 June 1984.